Sales

The Art Of Conversation

Anyone Can Say YES

By Zach Raymond

Copyright © 2015

ALL RIGHTS RESERVED.

No part of this publication may be reproduced or transmitted in any form whatsoever, electronic or mechanical, including photocopying, recording, or by any informational storage or retrieval system without express written, dated and signed permission from the author.

Description

The world of sales is a jungle compared to the rest of the world. To many, it doesn't seem as though it would be too difficult of a challenge to be a salesman, but the truth of the matter is that it is a difficult, yet rewarding job.

Rewarding, that is, if you are a good salesman, and if you are making those sales. For many people who are working on commission, they need to make those sales if they hope to bring home a decent paycheck, otherwise, they are looking at slim pickings for the next pay period.

Few people realize that there is a real knack to being an effective salesman. They wrongly assume that all you need to do is call people or knock on their doors and toss the item in their face, then they will have no choice but to happily purchase whatever it is you have to offer.

For those that are struggling in the sales business, however, the world of sales is a much harder, more unforgiving place. If you don't get and keep your client's interest in a very short amount of time, that is, unfortunately, the end of the line for you, and you are left with no choice but to hit the road and hope for a better outcome next time.

Don't worry, there is light at the end of this tunnel, and there is hope for you, no matter what your sales situation is. This book is designed to help you in the most crucial part of your sales... the conversation.

Teaching you skills that are going to help you for your entire career, including:

- Body language skills
- Speech skills
- The key to being an effective speaker
- Landing that sale
- Keeping consistent numbers
- The skills needed to sell anything to anyone, at any time

Table of Contents

Description 3

Table of Contents 5

Introduction 8

Chapter 1 – Getting Started: The Magic of Conversation 12

   The art of conversation 13

   Study your client and meet them on their level. 15

Chapter 2 – Ambushing Your Target: Perfect Conversation ... 18

   The five key points to highly effective conversation. 19

   Friendliness 21

   Keep it casual 22

   Persuasion 23

   Optimism 25

   Persistence 27

Chapter 3 – How to Sell Things the Right Way 30

Make it personal 31

Have the answers 32

Fit your product into your customer's life 33

Chapter 4 – How To Be A Conversation Leader 36

Leading a conversation silently 37

Reverse psychology questions 38

Rhetorical questions 40

Chapter 5 – You Had Me At "Hello" 42

Attitude is everything 43

In person salesmen 44

Over the phone sales associate 46

Chapter 6 – How To Sell Ice To An Eskimo 49

Chapter 7 – The Salesman Personality 55

Adopt the salesman personality 57

But how do I develop these qualities? 58

Practice makes perfect 60

Chapter 8 – Closing it Up: How to Land a Sale Every Time 61

Closing 61

Always keep up the assumption that they are going to make a purchase 63

Value your customer's time 63

Wish your client a good day 64

End on a positive note, even if the conversation didn't go well
.... 65

Wrapping it up with grace and ease... and landing that sale
.... 66

Conclusion 67

Introduction

Customers come and go, you call everyone on your calling list, and you are met time after time with the same statement. "Don't call me again", or, "please remove me from your calling list", and the list goes on.

Maybe you had no choice, and you had to become a salesman out of necessity. Now, here you are, trying to get that sale and make that commission, only to be met with discouragement after discouragement.

Or maybe, you really wanted to be a salesman, and maintain a classic job in the modern day world… only to question whether or not that was your calling after all. You try and try, and you are met with one 'no' after another.

This is all very discouraging, especially for someone who really wants... or needs... to be making those sales. It seems as though no matter what you do, you are never going to make those sales like you need to make them, thus keeping you trapped in a vicious cycle of phone call after phone call.

"There has got to be a better way," you tell yourself. You know that there are people out there who not only make a living at being a salesman, but also make a lot of money by doing it. It seems like they just have a knack of knowing how to relate to people, and how to say the right thing and make people feel as though they can't live without the product.

Are these salesman gifted? Do they know something that you don't? How do they manage to keep everyone so interested in what they are selling, even if you yourself can see that it doesn't do them any more good to have the product than no to?

The answer to their success lies in one simple thing: their technique. There really is a technique to all of this that makes or breaks a sale. You do have to know what to say, when to say it, and how to say it. Just telling a potential customer about a product isn't enough, you have to tell them why they need it, and why their lives are going to be better if they have it.

This is a process that takes practice, and you are going to have to work to perfect your own unique style. There are universal laws that you can follow that will land you your sale, but you have to also learn how to make it your own.

This book is going to walk you through these universal laws, and it is also going to show you how to make these things your own. In no time at all you are going to develop your own unique salesman style, and you will be out there on the field selling anything that you are given to sell.

It doesn't matter what your social skills are, whether you are shy, whether you are good at talking to strangers, or anything like that. All you need is a little bit of knowledge, and a lot of practice, and you are going to be one of the best salesman around.

Get ready, by the end of this book, you are going to be a whole new salesman, and your sales are going to be through the roof!

Chapter 1 – Getting Started: The Magic of Conversation

There are salesman and women around us all day long. We get calls from them, we see them on the television, rarely, we even see them on our own doorsteps… and the list goes on.

When we see these men and women, we tend to have our answer already lined up in our brains. We don't want what they have to sell, no matter what it is, or how they intend to sell it.

In a certain realm, the case is closed before it is even open. For those who are in the positions of the salesman, this can be really difficult. Then, there are the less obvious salesmen.

These are the people that we see in malls and in our favorite department stores. They tend to point us in the direction of the thing we are after, or they happen to tell us just what we need to complete that look or that project.

We buy what they tell us to buy, but we never felt like they sold us anything...

The art of conversation

There is a real knack to conversing properly. It doesn't seem like this would be a big deal, but that is really the key difference between the two kinds of salesmen that we described above.

In the first scenario, we already had our minds made up about what the person was going to say, so we didn't give them a chance to say it. In the second situation, we were just going about our day, and the salesperson integrated themselves into what we were doing, met us on our level, and got us to buy what they wanted us to buy, all without us even realizing it.

So how did they do it? What was the key that they used? Conversation.

They showed an interest in what we were wearing, or doing, and they acted as though they wanted us to look our best, or succeed at our project. If you are going to be an effective salesman, you need to do this, too.

Study your client and meet them on their level.

Learn to watch your client. Read them, and find out what it is they are after. When you know what it is that they want, then you will be able to meet them there, and guide them to a sale, no matter what it is.

No matter what you are selling, no matter what your potential customer is doing, you can sell them what you have to sell. Granted, this is a hit and miss sort of situation, but that is the case in any retail world.

If you learn how to meet your customer on their level, and relate to them in a way that makes them feel worth your time and efforts, then they are going to respond in the way that you want them to respond. This is all really easy to do, if you have mastered the art of conversation.

But how do I know what they want? And how do I know how to engage them? I feel so intimidated when it comes to people, how am I going to address them in a way that makes them feel valuable?

These are all questions that tend to swirl through the first time salesman's mind. Of course it may feel intimidating at first, especially for those that are not outgoing or used to dealing with the public, but don't worry, there are specific questions for you to ask yourself, and things for you to ask your customer, that will lighten everything up and get you to where you want to be.

In addition to the questions that you need to ask yourself, there are also steps for you to follow. Simple things that are easy to do, they just need practice to be done right.

With some work and a little bit of consistency, these are things that are going to come second nature to you, and in no time at all you are going to be a world class salesman in any situation, and at a moment's notice.

Chapter 2 – Ambushing Your Target: Perfect Conversation

There are a lot of great things that come out of good conversation, and even better things come out of it for those that are in the sales business. If you are good at conversation already, you are in luck, as this will come second nature to you, but if you aren't that good at it, then here are some things that you can do that will help you develop your conversational skills.

The five key points to highly effective conversation.

We have all kinds of conversations throughout our day. The happy conversations, the business conversations, the simple, quick, in the middle of the shopping mall conversations, and so on.

There are basic elements that certain conversations have in common. The conversations that you have with friends or loved ones are going to be vastly different from the conversations you have with your hairdresser, and the conversation you have with her is different still from the ones you have with the cashier at the grocery store.

When it comes to sales, you need to learn the five things that all sales conversations have in common, and what you can incorporate into yours to make them the most effective that they can be.

1. Friendliness
2. Casualness
3. Persuasion
4. Optimism
5. Persistence

These are simple things in and of themselves, and may seem to be insignificant, but they are key when it comes to effective sales conversations, and you are going to need to master each and every point.

Let's go through each of them now, and take a closer look at how you can use them in your conversations.

Friendliness

Being friendly is the most important part of a sales conversation. As soon as you appear rude, in a hurry, or in any way higher than the customer, you are going to lose them. A customer wants someone who is able to relate to them, and someone who cares about what their needs are.

If you want to be an effective salesman, you need to learn how to meet your customer where they are. Ask yourself what you would want if you were in their position. Would you want someone who has the answers? Would you want someone who is able to give you more advice?

Once you know what you would want, you are going to be better able to give your customer what they would want.

Keep it casual

Make sure you keep a no pressure, no worry environment when you are talking to your customer. You don't want them to feel pressured, or you are apt to lose them. Make them feel as though you have all the time in the world for them, even if you don't.

Answer their questions, multiple times, if necessary, and make sure they are getting the information that they need. Suggest things that are relevant and useful to them, and don't be so worried about how quickly they are moving towards a purchase.

As long as you have a customer on the line, then you have hope of making a sale, so don't push them. When they feel that they are in a pressured situation, they are likely to leave without making a purchase, and the fastest way to make them feel pressured is to hurry them along.

To add to the casual tone, ask questions about them, and their lives. Keep it nice, simple and casual.

Persuasion

Another big key point to a sales conversation is persuasion. You need to be able to convince your customer that what you have to sell is the best thing that they could possibly get, or that they can't be happy unless they purchase that item from you.

You need to have knowledge about what you are selling, and add to that knowledge suggestions on how your product will make your client's life better.

Example:

You are a sales associate in a clothing store and you see a young woman trying on belts. She is wearing a skirt and a sweater, and boots. Now, you can go up to her and offer to show her different belts, but you can see that she is already there, so it is likely that is what she is going to buy.

As a sales associate, it would be better for you if you were able to sell her more than what she intended, and to do that, you are going to need to persuade her. To do this, you need to point her in the direction of something that will compliment her outfit, yet not be obvious about it.

Suggest to her that she purchase a new scarf, or earrings, or perhaps a hand bag. These are things that will go with what she is wearing, and if you portray them as the perfect addition to her outfit, she is going to be a lot more likely to want to purchase it.

These are things that do take some practice to achieve, but you can do it if you are careful to time it right, and keep it casual.

Optimism

It is a well-known fact that those that are optimistic attract people, and this is crucial for a sales associate. You want to draw people in, no matter what you are trying to sell, and the best way to do that is to be bright and cheery.

People aren't going to be drawn to you if you look like your dog just died, and they aren't going to want to buy anything at all if they feel like you are having the worst day ever.

It is remarkable how your attitude will affect the attitudes of those that are buying from you. There are a lot of subliminal feelings that people are able to pick up on through things such as your body language, your attitude, and your overall demeanor.

When you are speaking with a potential buyer about anything, act as though this is the best move they could possibly be making, and act thrilled that you get to be a part of this with them. If they feel that there is someone out there that has absolutely no doubt about what they are doing, then they are going to be a lot more likely to want to purchase the item from you than if they are doubtful it is a good idea.

You have to be the biggest cheerleader for your customers, and you need to make them believe that this is a good option for them. The more convincing you are that this is a good option, the more likely they are going to be to make that move.

No matter what, even if they refuse to purchase what you are selling, be a person that views the glass as half full, and the day as one that is full of opportunity. You want to leave them with a good feeling, if they don't buy something from you the first time you meet, that doesn't mean that they won't be back.

Persistence

Persistence is a trait that you need to learn how to use properly. There is a fine line between being persistent and being annoying, and you don't want to cross the line into the other realm.

A persistent associate is one that is more flirty than not, and one that genuinely seems to feel that the item is going to better the customer's life. An annoying associate is one that is clearly just trying to make a sale, and one that is going to be after money first and foremost.

While it is true that as a salesman you do want to make the sale, you don't want that to appear evident to your customer. They know that you are trying to sell them something, but when it seems like money is all that matters, they are turned off by the attitude and may not purchase anything at all.

You as a sales associate are supposed to draw in business from your customer. This means that you need to make them feel like it is all about them, and that paying you is nothing but a minor side effect that happens from them getting what is going to make their life even better than it already is.

Practice these points, and learn how to use them. I wish I could give you a perfect formula as to when and where to use them, but your conversations are all unique. As you develop your skills, you are going to learn where and when to use them to make the most out of your conversation.

You are going to learn the right way to use these points, but that is going to take time. Don't get discouraged when during the process, it is only a matter of time before you know exactly how to handle it.

Chapter 3 – How to Sell Things the Right Way

It may sound surprising, but there are right and wrong ways to sell things. We touched on this a little bit in the last chapter when we looked at the attitude a sales associate needs to have, but there is more to it than that.

Make it personal

When you are selling anything, no matter what it is, you need to be personal. If you have it, or if you have used it in the past, that is even better. If you haven't, then you need to learn what you can about the product so you can then answer questions your customers have.

If you don't know what you are selling, how are you going to be able to stand by it? When your customer is buying something from you, they trust that you are selling them an item that is quality, and that is going to last. If you don't even know what it is, how are they going to trust that it is going to last?

If you can, use examples of times when you used the product, or when someone you know used it. Be specific, and be real. Even if it is a fictional story, you need to make it convincing enough they are going to believe you. Don't have any far-fetched tale of something that happened to a friend of a friend, rather, be detailed, and have a story that actually makes sense.

The more your customer feels like they are a part of this story, or the more that they feel they can use the product in their own life, the more likely it is you are going to make that sale.

Have the answers

Before you sell anything, you need to know what people are asking about it. Know what they want to know, so to speak. If you don't know what that is, try looking at the FAQ page. Learn what they are asking, and learn the answers.

Learn the flaws. While it is important to sell a product that you stand behind, and one that you can assure your customer is going to last, you do need to know what the issues have been with the product. There are several benefits to this, as you can then offer troubleshooting advice, preventative measures, and other technical difficulties and fixes that you may run across with the product.

Fit your product into your customer' s life

When your customer is looking to purchase a product, whether they have specifically come to you or not, you need to make them feel that they can use what you are selling. Fit your product into their lives, and show them that they can use it in a number of ways.

At a loss on how to do this? Consider trying these methods:

1. Give them specific suggestions on how to use the product

2. Give them a visual of where the product would be in their home

3. Make it sound as though the product is just what they need to have fun

4. Make them feel that the product is going to make them happy

5. Give them an idea of how you can relate, and how this product changed that for you

When people feel that you know what they need, they open up a lot more, and you are going to feel a lot more comfortable having conversations with them. This is all a cycle that is going to work out for the best for you, as the more comfortable you feel in a conversation, the more you are going to want to guide it.

This is when you are able to draw in the five key points to any sales conversation, and before you know it, you are going to be selling your product.

Chapter 4 – How To Be A Conversation Leader

As a sales associate, you need to have a passive aggressive manner of conversation. This means that you need to lead the conversation, but you need to do it in a way that makes your client feel as though they are the ones leading the conversation.

Now, a key thing to remember when it comes to being a leader in conversation is to remember that it doesn't matter who is doing the talking. Some people mistakenly believe that in order to be a conversation leader, you need to be the one who is doing all the talking.

That is far from the truth. To be a conversation leader, you need to be in control of where the conversation is going, even if you aren't talking much at all.

Leading a conversation silently

You do need to say some things if you are going to lead the conversation, and of course you are going to need to talk if you are going to sell something to anyone, but you do need to remember that there is a way to lead a conversation and only say very few words.

To do this, you need to learn how to ask the right questions. There isn't a list of questions for you to ask as there is for the key points of conversation, but rather, there are a couple kinds of questions that you need to ask in order to gain control of the conversation.

These are:

1. Reverse psychology questions
2. Rhetorical questions

There is a lot of power in these kinds of questions, and they are great for what you need when it comes to leading a conversation in a passive manner. Now, you need to know the difference between these kinds of questions, and how they can effectively help you.

Reverse psychology questions

These are questions that make the customer feel as though they are making the decision, even though you already know what they are going for. To do these, you need to offer your client a deal, but make them feel as though you would rather they went with something else.

As a sales associate, you will find that even the best client is still going to be on their guard when it comes to you, so they are going to go with what they feel is best. There is a trick to this, as you want them to go with the offer that you have set up, but you should still offer them an alternative, that they are unlikely to go for, yet that will make them feel as though they are making a better decision.

Example:

You want your client to purchase the gold pack, it sells for a little more than the other one, but the other one doesn't last as long. Of course you want them to go with the gold, but you need to make the silver sound just good enough, except focus on the fact that it doesn't last as long.

You will find that your clients are going to be more inclined to go with the gold pack, which is what you wanted, even though you were pressing them to go for the silver.

Rhetorical questions

These are questions that don't require an answer, and the reason they are so good for your sales pitch is because you make the client feel as though they are in complete control of the situation.

Ask them questions that will make them feel as though they are getting the best thing out there, but phrase the question in a light that doesn't require an answer.

1. "Of course you will be going with the best available?"

2. "Obviously insured for the full year, we wouldn't want it breaking down on month 10 now, would we?"

3. "Clearly you would want that in a combo, that is the best deal, after all?"

You will get the hang of asking rhetorical questions. They do take a bit of practice to get the hang of, but when you do, you will see how effective they are at controlling a conversation.

As soon as you ask one, your customer is going to feel like they are the ones in control. They will feel that they do deserve the best, and that there isn't a way that they would go for anything less.

You may act as though you are trying to save them money with a smaller product, or like it would be in their best interest to go with something that wasn't quite as good, but at that point, they are going to want the best of the best, and there will be little that can change their mind.

As the sales associate, this is what you want, you just can't let on that this is what you want. It goes back to the reverse psychology, and the more your client feels that they are in control, the better.

Chapter 5 – You Had Me At " Hello"

Few of us realize that there is great importance in the greeting. When it comes to selling an item, you need to make a killer first impression, every time. It has been scientifically proven that people form opinions about people that they meet within 5 seconds of meeting them.

Now, don't worry about the pressure, and yes, we do admit that puts on a lot of pressure, but there is no need to stress about it. When you know you are going to be in control of the conversation, it becomes easy to open it up.

Attitude is everything

When it comes to the first impression, you need to be careful. There are two ways you are going to have to deal with this:

1. In person
2. Over the phone

There tends to be only two kinds of sales associates these days, those that are in the store and face to face with the customers, and those that are over the phone. Now, it is obvious the face to face people are going to have an advantage in this realm, but that isn't any reason for the over the phone salesman to get discouraged, there is plenty of hope for them as well.

In person salesmen

You can't be arrogant. That is the biggest turn off in the world. When you are approaching a potential customer, you need to be confident, friendly, and outgoing, but never arrogant. The more you seem to be above the customers, the less they are going to want to engage you.

Smile. Practice a nice smile in front of the mirror. This is something that is going to be a major selling point to the client. If they see you smile as you walk up, they are likely to smile back, and the tone of the conversation is going to be a lot more relaxed than it would be otherwise.

Maintain eye contact. You need to have the confidence to hold the eye contact of your customers. There is a level of trust that comes out of eye contact, and if you are able to hold their gaze, you are going to find that they are a lot more likely to purchase something from you.

Body language. Keep your arms unfolded, and have an open attitude. There is something closed off about folding your arms, and if you have a habit of folding them over your chest, you are going to appear a lot less friendly than if you kept them resting at your side.

While these are all things that you can easily practice at home, it is helpful to ask a friend or family member to help you out if you need some feedback. It can be hard to know what you are actually doing when you are speaking with someone, as your focus will shift to them and off of what you are currently doing.

Over the phone sales associate

While you are at a bit of a disadvantage when it comes to over the phone pitching, you are not at a total loss. There are still things that you can do that will engage your client and help you land that all important sale.

Smile. Yes, even though you are talking to them over the phone, it is important that you smile. You can hear it in a person's voice when they are smiling, and it is something that your clients will be able to pick up on.

Let them speak. As a sales associate, especially one that is dealing over the phone, you need to make sure you are giving your customer time to speak. It is tempting to get your speech out and in the open, but your client may feel that they are being rushed or ignored if you do that.

Give them time to speak, and acknowledge what they are saying. After they have spoken their peace, you are free to speak yours.

Be human. It is hard to maintain that conversationalist tone when you say the same thing over and over again, but when you are dealing with a person over the phone, you need to make sure you are treating them with as much enthusiasm as you did the first client that you called.

Sure, to you this is client number 100, but to them, you are the first, and they want to be treated as though they are the first. Make sure you are keeping up your enthusiasm, and you talk to the first client as you would talk to the last client on your list, and vice versa.

You never know which one is going to buy from you, and you don't want to lose out on a client because the person that you had to call before them was rude to you.

As a general rule of thumb, take a deep breath before you dial the next number, and you are always going to have that smile when you talk to each and every client. There is a high level of patience that is required for this sort of work, but if you are able to pull it off, you are going to find that it is even more rewarding than dealing with clients face to face.

The key to conversation really is the introduction, so take the time to make your 'hello' fun, clear, and inviting.

Chapter 6 – How To Sell Ice To An Eskimo

There is a famous saying used to describe salesmen that are really good at what they do… it is said that these men can sell ice to an Eskimo. Why this is so funny is that when you are in Alaska, or anywhere up North, there is so much snow and ice, that is the last thing that you are going to need, yet it is said that this person can sell ice to these people.

Of course it is nothing more than a figure of speech, but it gets the point across quite nicely. That is exactly the kind of salesman that you want to be, and that is what we are shooting for when we are giving you the steps in this book.

Being a salesman is a delicate job. You need to do things that aren't entirely necessary, or at least make things that aren't necessary to a person sound very necessary to that person. Make them believe that it is the greatest thing that ever was.

As we have seen in the previous chapters, a lot of this comes from conversation. There is more to it than that, of course, but conversation has a lot to do with it. Now, let's take a look at the other factors that come with a good salesman. We have seen that they are good at opening a conversation, that they are good at keeping the person interested, and that they have a good overall body language, but what about the product itself?

There has to be some good in that, or nobody would buy it... or does there?

Many sales associates make the mistake of pressing the product too hard, and thus losing a sale. When you are a salesman, you want to make sales. Of course you want the customer to be happy with the product, and it is largely your job to make sure they feel that they will be, but at the end of the day, you need to make a sale more than you need to sell the product.

Just as an Eskimo has no use for ice, you don't need to necessarily target a specific person with a specific product. In order to get someone to buy anything, you need to appeal to their imagination. Play on what they wish they were, or what they want to be.

It doesn't have to be anything huge or elaborate, but if you can make a housewife feel that she is one step closer to her dream of being a master chef by purchasing your set of knives, then you have done your job. If you can make a fisherman feel that he is that much closer to landing that major fish by buying your lure, then you are successful.

You see, you do want your client to be happy, but if you spent all of your time pushing your lure, you may not get the same clients that you would if you spent your time pushing that they would get a major catch if they went fishing with that lure.

What you are selling more than the product is the idea. The fantasy that what you are selling is exactly what they need to make what they want happen. This is why you see in the advertising on the television all of the pics of the 'before' models are vastly different than what happens in the 'after' models.

The media is good at making you feel like you are not good enough on your own, and thus you need to have this or that to make it better. While that is not your goal with each of your clients, you do want to emphasize all they need to be happy is that product you are selling.

There is a real trick to this that will take some time to master, but if you are consistent with your practice, and patient with how it is received, you will start to see the results that you want. You just have to be careful when you are practicing this to follow the other guides that we have set up.

Never get pushy, and never get bossy. You want to maintain that cool, calm, and collected attitude the entire time, and make sure the customer feels like they are in control, whether you are or they are.

When you finally master this trick, you are going to see that there are very few things that come by that you can't sell.

Chapter 7 – The Salesman Personality

We all have that person in our lives that we can't say 'no' to. Whatever they want, whether we want to do it or not, we agree to do, just because they asked. So what is it about that person that makes them irresistible?

Is it their attitude?

The way they look?

The way they act?

What is it?

It may come as a surprise to you, but the reason these people are so irresistible is a combination of those traits. Those people know what to say, and when to say it, and they do it well.

They know how you work, and what you need to hear in order to get you to do what they want you to do. The great thing about this is that you can figure out what your client needs to hear to get them to do what you want them to do.

Some would call it manipulation, others would call it skill. Whatever you want to call it, the end result is the same, and that is your customer buying your product, and maybe even coming back for more.

Adopt the salesman personality

You don't have to be a sales associate all the time, only when you are in the process of selling a product. There is some relief to this, as you can still be yourself more than anything, but you should learn how to adopt the salesman personality at a moment's notice.

Think of it as an actor getting into character for a scene. Develop the character that you want to be in your mind, then work to be that person when you need to be.

Here is a list of the standout qualities that a great salesman has:

1. An outgoing mindset
2. An agreeable manner
3. Talkative
4. Friendly
5. Happy

Whenever you picture in your mind that person that you can't say no to, odds are they have many if not all of these qualities, and once you are able to adopt them for yourself, you will also be a winning salesman.

But how do I develop these qualities?

Practice makes perfect whenever you are learning anything new, and the same goes for personality changes. This means that you need to put your new self into action, and the sooner the better.

If you aren't an outgoing person to begin with, the first thing that you need to do is develop your outgoing attitude. The best way to do this is to get out and get involved. The best way to do this is to start small.

Get out to your local supermarket, and as you are paying for your purchase, strike up a conversation with the cashier. If you do this often, it is going to get easier each time you do it.

When you are comfortable speaking to your cashier, move on to the people that are in line around you. Don't be afraid to say hello to anyone, but keep it in check... remember the second rule of being a good salesman is to be friendly and outgoing, and not annoying.

Another trick that you can do that will help you open up to the people around you is to *treat everyone that you meet like they are already your best friend.*

You are always happy to see your best friend, and you are always ready to chat it up, even if it is about nothing at all. If you treat everyone that you meet like this, you are going to find that you won't have any problems striking up a conversation with anyone that you meet.

Once you are able to approach anyone, you are going to find that you are able to talk to them about anything. This is going to make sales pitches go so much better, and make both your customer... and you... feel more at ease when you are talking to them about your product.

Practice makes perfect

Whatever you do, practice. The more you work at something, the better you are going to get at doing it. Let your anxiety melt away as you work on this, and as you develop your own unique persona, you will see how easy it is.

Chapter 8 – Closing it Up: How to Land a Sale Every Time

While all of these tips are very important when it comes to developing a winning salesman personality and mastering conversation skills, there is still one very important thing you need to master in order to succeed as a salesman.

Closing

The ending of the interaction is by far the most important part of the entire process. How you wrap up your conversation can be exactly what it takes for you to land your sale and bring it all home.

For many, this is the part when they feel awkward, or don't know what to say, so they fumble and drop the ball. When this happens, they throw a huge damper on the client, or they lose them all together.

When you are closing your conversation, there are a few things that you need to remember to do in order to finish out strong, and bring the interaction around full circle.

1. Wrap up the conversation with the assumption they are going to purchase

2. Thank your customer for their time and consideration

3. Wish them a good day

4. End on a positive note, even if the conversation didn't go well

Always keep up the assumption that they are going to make a purchase

Unless your client clear that they don't want to purchase the product from you, treat them as though they were going to make the purchase. If someone doesn't want an item, you are going to know it, and if you are shaky with your response, or treat them as though they aren't going to, you could lose them.

Value your customer's time

Remember that your customer's time is valuable, and they don't have to give you any of their time, so if you are selling to someone who has given you some of their time, thank them for doing so, and make sure they know that you appreciate it.

Wish your client a good day

You want to end your conversation focusing on your client, and the best way to do that is to bid them a good day. We don't realize how important it is to hear these words until someone doesn't say them to us, so make sure you remember to say them.

Your customer may not realize that you said that, but they are definitely going to notice if you don't. To make sure that you remember to say it, remember to make the entire conversation about your client. When the focus is on them, it is going to be a lot easier to remember to tell them to have a good day.

End on a positive note, even if the conversation didn't go well

You are going to run into all kinds of clients and potential customers in your day. It doesn't matter if you are an in person sales associate or if you are over the phone, you are going to see people in all kinds of moods, and you are going to be treated in many different ways.

For some, a sales person is a nuisance, and even though they should treat you with respect, they may not. Others are happy to speak with you whether or not they want to buy something... yet no matter how your conversation goes, you need to end it the same way.

Be kind, be positive, and be happy. There is nothing wrong with you, and you may have just caught your customer at a bad time. Whatever the case, you are doing your job well.

Wrapping it up with grace and ease... and landing that sale

This is going to take practice, but you are going to get better at it the more you work at it. The important thing is that you don't get discouraged, and that you stay happy and upbeat for the next person that you interact with.

The more comfortable you are with a conversation, the more it is going to shine through, and the more you are going to make those sales. The attitude of the sales associate really does have a major effect on sales, so you do need to do your part in making your client happy.

If you are consistent in your practice, and optimistic about the results, you are going to get better at what you do, and you are going to make consistent sales, no matter what you are selling.

Conclusion

There you have it. Everything you need to know to be the best salesman out there. If you follow these lessons, and work hard to perfect your skills, you are going to see a rise to your sales in no time, and your profits are going to come rolling in.

No matter what you were like when you started this book, whether or not you thought that you could do it, or what you are selling, these steps are going to help you overcome any fears that you may have when it comes to the public, and sharpen any skills that you need to make the sales that you need to be making.

Whatever you do, don't give up. The sales pitch is something that takes a while to develop, even if you are already good at it, so expect to spend some time on this before you are able to draw in any real customers.

Remember to follow the steps that we have provided, and to remain optimistic when you are working on them. These are things that change gradually, they don't happen overnight, so don't feel like you are doing anything wrong when you have to work at it.

Some of the results are immediate, others are going to take a little while for you to get the hang of them. The key to being a good salesman is to being upbeat and positive, even when you are in a rough spot. Keep your chin up, and you will see things always get better.

Persistence is key when it comes to sales. You don't have to harass your customers to buy, you need to harass yourself to be better. Don't ever reach a level in which you assume that you have arrived, or that you don't need to work at it any more.

In this growing and changing world, there are always going to be new things to sell, and new methods that you are going to need to use to sell them. Stay on top of the news and stay on top of your game, and you will notice that you are also on top of your sales.

You need to be willing to change and adapt with the times, and you will see that your work will reflect that. Stay passionate, and stay true to yourself, and you will become that salesman that you have always dreamed of being.

Can I Ask A Favor?

If you enjoyed this book, found it amazing or otherwise then I'd really appreciate it if you would post a short review on Amazon. I do read all the reviews personally so that I can continually write what people are wanting.

Thanks for your support!

Made in the USA
Monee, IL
02 January 2021